© Copyright 2017 Kay Brandt

Design and illustrations by
Kay Brandt.

Cover printed by
Nelson Printing, Saint Peter, Minnesota

Printed by
Crescent Publishing, Inc., Garretson, South Dakota

INTRODUCTION

It has been 30 years since I created my first garment. My mother's patience and encouragement made me a young accomplished seamstress. Being surrounded by grandmothers and aunts who had sewing rooms, it just seemed natural to me to spend much of my extra time sewing. Thanks to my mother for being such a great influence and patient teacher.

My sewing started out with Barbie dresses, then progressed quickly to clothing for me because selection for a petite girl in a rural area is limited. I had a full wardrobe before I went off to college. While in college for Illustration and Graphic Design, I had a great part-time job at a tailor shop. I had the privilege to work with an accomplished tailor, who had worked for Liberace. I also worked with a seamstress, who specialized in evening gowns. My skills were refined under their guidance and years of experience.

I continued sewing throughout my life for others and for myself. Later in life it was time to start a family. So I made a career change from full-time art director to part-time, self-employed seamstress. Working from home gave me the flexibility to garden, sew, paint/ illustrate and manage family time around my sewing.

After sewing bridal alterations for a few years - about one thousand dresses later - I began noticing many of the same issues over and over again with alterations and dress choice. Brides could have avoided some of these issues with some extra knowledge in sewing.

Knowing what to be aware of makes choosing a gown simpler and less stressful. Because sewing skills are typically no longer taught in school, I have prepared this guide to help make your choice in styles easier. This should save you money.

Gown Notes

Designer Model#/Name   How did it feel/fit? Cost$

____

____

____

____

____

____

____

____

____

____

____

Put on the gown and take a picture, look at it again later.

Try On All Styles.

Try On All Colors.

Take Pictures.

Every Body
Is Unique

CONTENTS

Bride

Special Ordering.............1
Styles........................1
Color.........................1
Heirloom......................2
Corset........................3
Savings for Bride.............3
Ordering/Measuring........4
How Tight.....................5
Hems..........................6
Petite Bride or Flats.........7
Hollowed Hem.................7
Rhinestone/Beading........8
Sides In.......................8
Boning........................9
Bra vs. Cup...................9
Undergarments...............10
Strapless Solutions.........11
Belting.......................13
Bustling......................13
Shoes.........................15
Jewelry.......................16
Tan Lines....................17
Hair/Veils...................18
Brides Emergency Diet..20

Bridesmaid

Style Considerations......21
Color..........................24
Money Saving Ideas......25

Junior Bridesmaid

Style Considerations......26

Mother

Style Considerations......28

Flower Girl

Style Considerations......29

Ring Bearer

Style Considerations......30

Groom

Style Considerations......30

Miscellaneous

Website Purchasing........31
Invitations....................31
Church/Venue
Considerations...............32
Holiday Weddings..........33
Destination Weddings....33
Measurements...............34

Bride

Special Ordering   Please note
that special ordering of your bridal gown
takes time. Six months is the average
shipping time. If you allow for less time
than that, you may incur a rush charge at
the bridal shop. You also have less time for
alterations. There could be another rush
charge.

Styles: Try All Styles.   You may be surprised what you
actually like at the shop. Take a picture and look at them later.
In the future, re-try on the gowns that flatter you most and that
make you feel comfortable and gorgeous.

*Many brides have made comments on their chosen gown style
not being what they expected or were looking for initially.*

Color: Try All Colors.   When trying on
gowns take a picture. Try taking the pictures by
a window for natural lighting so as to get the
true color on you if you can. White, ivory,
cream, oyster, sandstone, champagne and
more colors are
available. There are
great warm, neutral
and cool tones to
choose from.

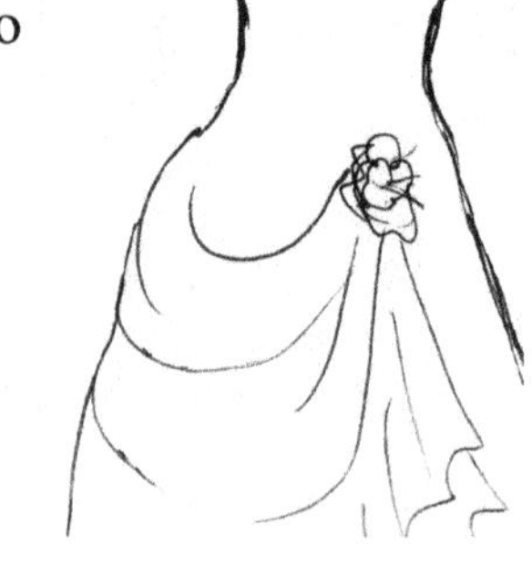

*On a lace dress, consider the satin
underlay to be a shade darker to 'show-
off/enhance' the lace detail. This will
compliment the lace pattern better in
your photos.*

Heirloom Dresses

Combining Old Or New Dresses is a great idea depending on the quality of the fabric and thread. Consider how many seams need to be reinforced and or recreated.

Older Gowns: Any damage? Typically you can wash the gown lightly by hand with a light soap like Ivory dish soap or other gentle hand wash detergents. You may need to wash/rinse several times until the water is clear. Lay gown on towels and roll it up, squeeze and unroll. Hang dry carefully in house on padded hanger with a fan blowing by it. If all looks fine, then go for it! Be wary of synthetic acetate/taffeta as it can stain easily from washing if not rinsed enough and perfectly hung to dry. Place a towel below for it to drip dry onto.

New Gowns: Revamping is great and can be timely. Discuss ideas and options with your seamstress and get the estimates written down to compare to other options later.

Delicate heirloom dress work takes time. Time is money. Discuss the cost and all options with your seamstress.

Your Gown Is A Future Heirloom. You can use the train from your gown to create a baptismal gown, or you can use the older gowns to make the baptismal gown.

Here is an example of a gown from the 1980s. Recreate the bodice for an updated look.

Another example with both bodice and hemline change.

Savings For The Bride

Get A Steal On A Dress - Consignment shop hunting. Also, consider checking out dry cleaners, for dresses that were not picked up. Or oder an evening gown that you tried on and love in white/ivory at that dress shop or store.

To Corset Or Not To Corset?

Reasons To Corset
- You love the look!
- Your body fluctuates sizes during times of stress. There is 1-3" of give and take in a corset dress!
- You are taking steroid medications for a medical condition making weight fluctuate.
- You have just given birth shortly before the wedding date.
- Your zipper styled dress is too small, and there is nothing left to let out anymore. Remove the zipper and have a corset created for the dress! Boning and loops will be added where the zipper was. A back panel of similar fabric will be attached and corset ribbon of similar matching fabric will be created.

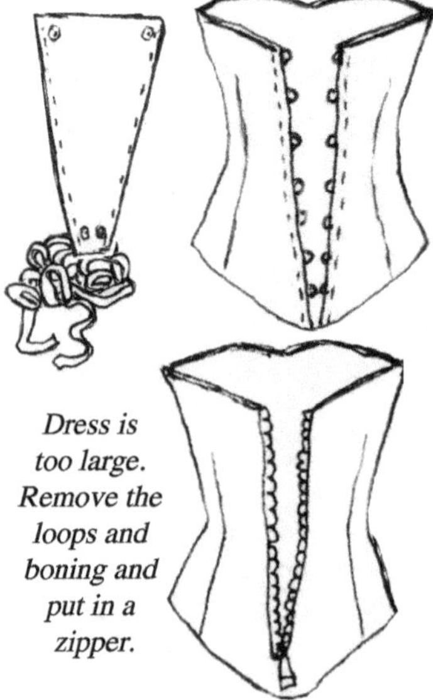

Dress is too small. Remove the zipper and put in loops, boning, back panel and satin ribbon.

Dress is too large. Remove the loops and boning and put in a zipper.

Reasons Not To Corset
- The look is just not for you or maybe the dress is on a limited special price and would fit you if the corset was removed. Price to put in zipper could range around $60-$200 depending on style.
- You do not want to rely on someone to lace you up properly.

Reasons To Remove Corset
- Your Corset Dress Is All Too Big, 6 sizes or more too big or you lost lots of weight. Take out the corset and put in an invisible zipper. Then alter the side seams also for a proper fit.

Ordering And Measurements

Usually Takes Six Months To Arrive. Go by the manufacturer's size chart. Size can vary between different countries and different manufacturers.

Fitted Bodice And Waist Only With A Gathered/ Full Skirt. Go by the largest of the chest and waist measurements. The dress is so full at the hips you do not need to go by your hip measurement as the dress is only fitted at waist and chest. The dress is not tight at the hips since it is fully gathered at the waist.

Fit bodice and waist dress.

Fit And Flare: Fitted Chest, Waist And Thighs. Go by the largest of the chest/waist/hips measurements. Hip ease in gown is most important to get your dress up to sit and go to the restroom. There is typically no extra lace fabric to 'let-out' the hip area as in the waist and chest, so the hip measurement is very important on lace gowns.

Body measurements should be taken at the bridal shop. See and agree with what the tape measure is saying at your chest, waist and hips and sign off on those measurements when ordering.

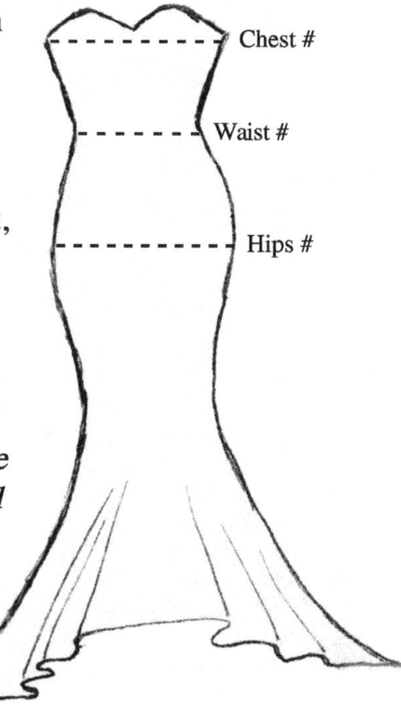

Fit and flare dress.

How Tight Is Too Tight Around The Thighs?

Considerations On Fit & Flare Or Mermaid Style:
- Can you sit down?
- Can you get the dress up when you use the ladies room?

What If You Can't Sit Or Can't Lift Up Your Dress, But You Like It That Tight Anyhow? Don't stress yourself out relying on bridesmaids to always be close at hand to help you get out of your dress for your restroom needs. You then should get bladder control pads, such as Poise Pads to avoid an accident.

Letting out the gown? There is fabric at chest typically and waist, but there is very little lace at the knee/thigh area.

What's In A Hem?

Many layers of varied fullness and fabrics!

Consider how many layers to be hemmed and the fabric type.

Straight Lace Edge Trim   Of 2" or less can be economical depending on how easy it is to remove/cut-off and re-attach at the new length. Or order dress with trim separate.

Lace Medallion/Scalloped Trim Of 3"-12":   Hem is pricier. It involves an intricate lace trim of varied pattern depths to be cut off and re-attached up higher. There is lots of preparation, extra fitting and the lace is then typically sewn on with many stitches on delicate fabric. Lots of time is needed to relocate and sew the intricate lace carefully back on.

Satin/Silk: Most economical hem. Typically a rolled hem or satin is lined and has horsehair at bottom to keep a smooth look. WRINKLES? How prone to wrinkles is the fabric of the satin or silk gown? To determine this you simply grab a handful of the fabric and squeeze for a few seconds and then let go. How many wrinkles do you see? Some satins are terrible with major wrinkle lines, others not too bad. Silk fabric usually has a mini-wrinkle look to it; if you like this look that is just fine.

Here is an example of a gown with five layers to hem.
- *Liner closest to body*
- *Tulle layer to puff-out skirt*
- *Liner on top of tulle*
- *Satin liner*
- *Top lace layer*

Tulle: Is inexpensive. Each layer can be cut with a rotary cutter to keep a smooth edge look.

Sheers: Fairly economical. Involves a rolled hem.

Satin With Horsehair Trim: Fairly economical. Involves removing the stitches and moving up horsehair trim and re-sewing it back on the satin.

Tulle Can/Can Puff: Inexpensive. Can usually be hemmed once at the thigh area of the can/can liner where all the layers meet and is done in one seam instead of many more hems.

Interior Liner: Economical. Involves a rolled hem.

Is The Bride Petite Or Wearing Flats?

Order the hollowed hem if very ornate lace trim on the hem   .
Alterations to a lace-trimmed or beaded hem is usually more expensive. Order to the proper length with shoes on. Designer/manufacturer hem length are based on an average to tall woman who is also wearing 4" heels. Order the hollowed hem - I really suggest it - because the initial upfront hollowed charge for the proper length is much less than if the seamstress has to relocate the ornate lace.

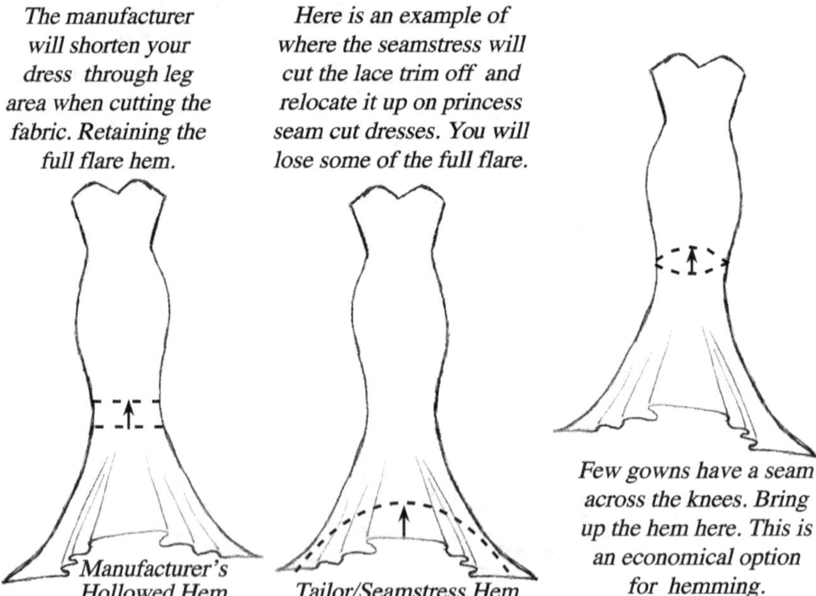

Rhinestone/Bead Caution

It is shiny gorgeous. I like the bling. Great light reflectors and excellent accents for the front of the gown. Rhinestones can, however, snag onto loose woven furniture and onto some sweaters when hugging guests. They can also rub your under-arm raw. Move your arms a lot in the sample dress. Armpits/underarm areas may get tender if there are too many rhinestones rubbing. Either avoid a gown with many rhinestones at the sides or have some removed on the sides in the tender area.

Many layers of the gown may be taken in by the sewing machine, but not the shell (outer layer). The seamstress must remove the rhinestones by hand first, then sew the fabric by machine, then re-attach the rhinestones by hand to cover up the side seam. Hand sewing takes more time which adds cost to alterations.

Taking In The Sides Need to tighten the chest? And/or ribs? And/or waist? And/or hips? And/or thighs?

Cost is determined by how many layers of fabric need to be taken in. Beads, lace, tulle overlays, satin liners and more can make for four to ten or more layers, which greatly affects the cost. Gowns vary from four to sixteen side seams or more. Most lace overlays

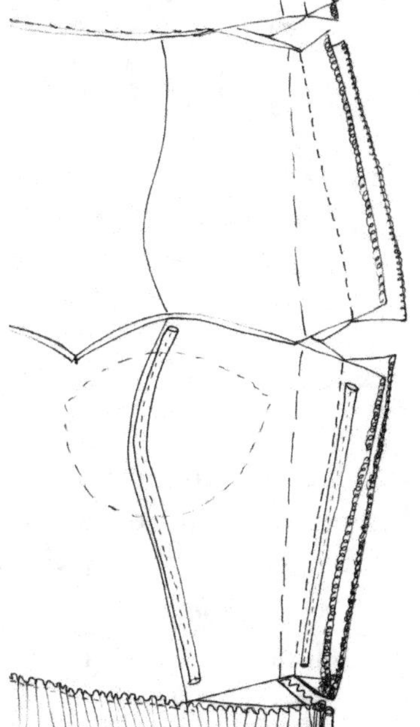

The dress marked before sides being taken in.

The dress sides after being taken in. The top sides by bust will be re-sloped.

An inside view of the side seams being taken in and waistline re-attached.

must be done by hand. All beadwork is done by hand. Consider this if cost is an issue on a dress that will most likely need lots of altering.

Regular side seam.

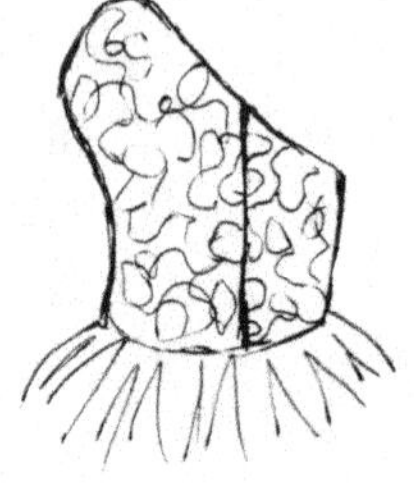

Regular side seam with lace.

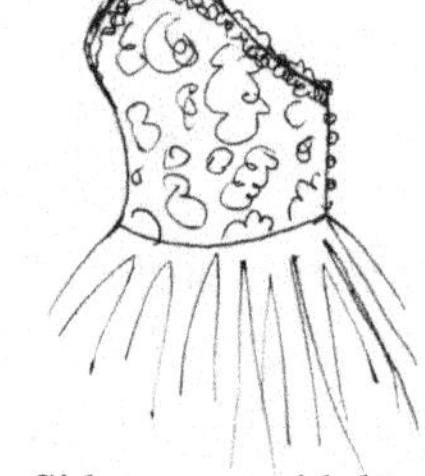

Side seams with lace overly piecing on top to hide the side seam.

Boning Additions

Do your sides on the gown look bumpy? Your gown may not have any boning on the sides. You can add boning to give structure and to keep the fabrics more smooth. Also, if your chest seems to be weighing down the front of the gown, you may need to add boning in the chest on the "princess lines" of the liner of the gown. You can also add boning to your corset panel if it is not staying smooth along your back.

Bra Versus Cups

Bras come in many styles: Strapless at rib cage, strapless to waist, and strapless to under belly. Many bras can make skin pressure ridges on our bodies. Some may push up your chest too much, like it is on a shelf, creating a crease atop your chest. Avoid this. You may be able to see all the undergarment ridges in soft/slinky gowns. In other dresses, you may be fine in your bra and undergarments if you can not see them. If you find it comfortable, then go for it.

Typically, once the dress is tailored to fit your bodice properly you will not need to wear a bra. If there is still room between your chest and the dress after the gown fits you perfectly in the bodice, use cups to 'lift-up' your chest to get rid of any 'peak-a-boo' open areas. Avoid cups that are too large because you do not want a crease on the top of your chest.

I prefer cups. Cups are a better fit, and do not make pressure ridges like a bra can. They do not slide down after a long day like a strapless bra. They are also cooler to wear than a bra. Cups can be tacked in between the shell and lining of the dress or just on top of the inner lining. There are many sizes and depths of padding available in cups.

Under Garments

If your gown is only two to three layers of a soft slinky satin you may want to consider lacey underwear. Try scalloped trimmed lacey boy-short panties to avoid a visible seam on waist and legs. Most should avoid body shapers. Body shapers are great for smoothing out rolls around the torso only. Body shapers simply relocate your flesh to other areas. Depending on the type of body shaper you may get visible body lines (flesh bulges) on the thighs, around the waist and around the underarms which can create a "bulging" effect. This can be quite visible on a soft smooth dress.

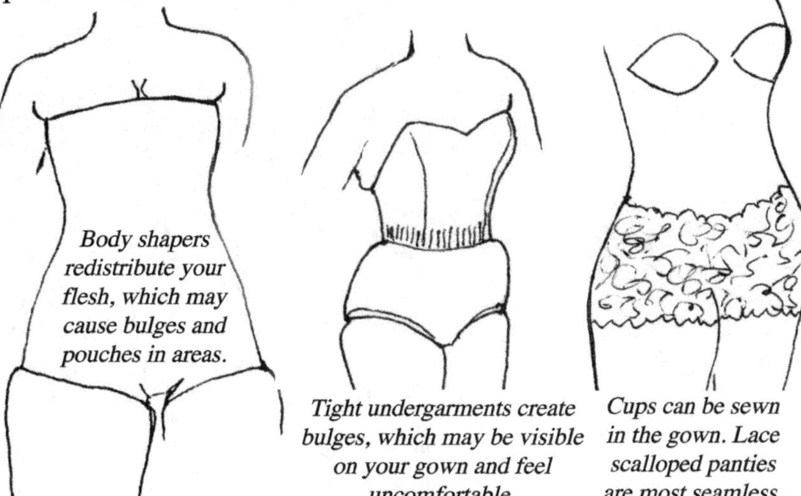

Body shapers redistribute your flesh, which may cause bulges and pouches in areas.

Tight undergarments create bulges, which may be visible on your gown and feel uncomfortable.

Cups can be sewn in the gown. Lace scalloped panties are most seamless.

Solutions For Your Strapless Gown

There are many ways to add support or a different style to your strapless gown.

Cap Sleeves Or Straps: Some designers are now offering sew-on cap sleeves with lace and beading that coordinate with some of the strapless gowns. Prices and styles vary. Plus some designers also offer the option to purchase the coordinating lace fabric or satin which can be used to create straps, halters, sleeves, etc. Also you can play with other fabrics from home or store! Try a scarf, buy lace or trim, or embellished ribbon belting, etc. and see what looks complimentary to the gown. Matching the color of the satin is the most important as it is most obvious in photos. The lace fabrics scallop pattern should be complimentary in similar pattern if not matching. Color needs to match.

A cautionary point for women with larger busts is that a thin halter or shoulder straps may end up giving you a terrible neck ache and or a pinched look. Also, some decorative metal belts may start out looking great as a shoulder strap, but could be a problem because the metal ends may dig deep into your skin. Line it with ribbon to soften for skin comfort.

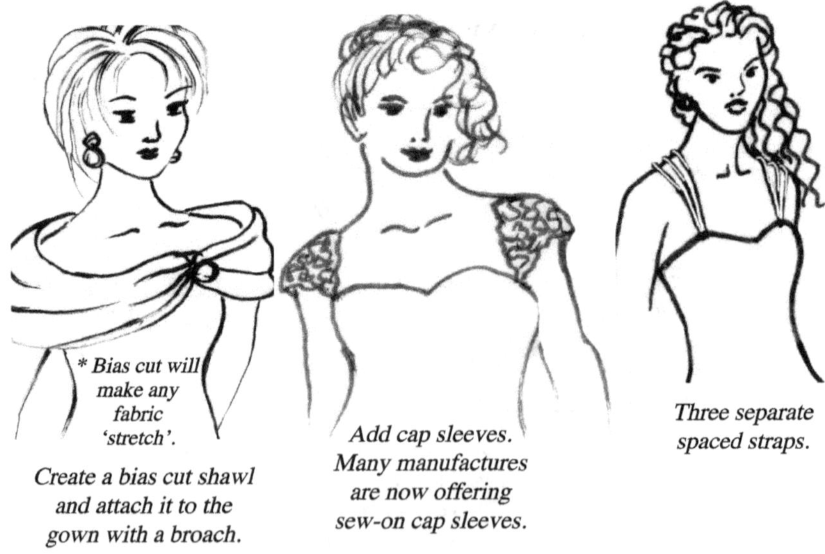

Bias cut will make any fabric 'stretch'.

Create a bias cut shawl and attach it to the gown with a broach.

Add cap sleeves. Many manufactures are now offering sew-on cap sleeves.

Three separate spaced straps.

Strap Options

Belting

Adding a ribbon with flowers or a beaded belt is a nice touch. Have it tacked at the sides and by the front embellishment if there is one. Add belting to help balance your added sleeves or straps on the gown. On corset gowns, the ribbon belt can be sewn into the edges of the corset so as to have no bow/belt line in the back of the gown if you desire.

"Bubble" bustle.

All around bustle, great if planning to wear flats from heels, keeps from tripping on front hem as well as back.

Bustled at zipper end, great for showcasing the trim on the hem.

Bustling

Why Bustle?   After the ceremony your guests will be all around you. If left un-bustled, someone will step on your dress, getting it dirty, ripping it and also possibly causing you to fall. Bustling keeps the dress up off the floor surface so that no one steps on your dress, which keeps the fabric clean, and keeps the dress from essentially being a mop to the floor. It also makes dancing easier.

**The hanging hook on the liner of the gown is not designed for nor is strong enough for bustling. No dress comes with bustle hooks unless it is previously worn.*

** The fuller the dress, the more bustling sets will be needed.*

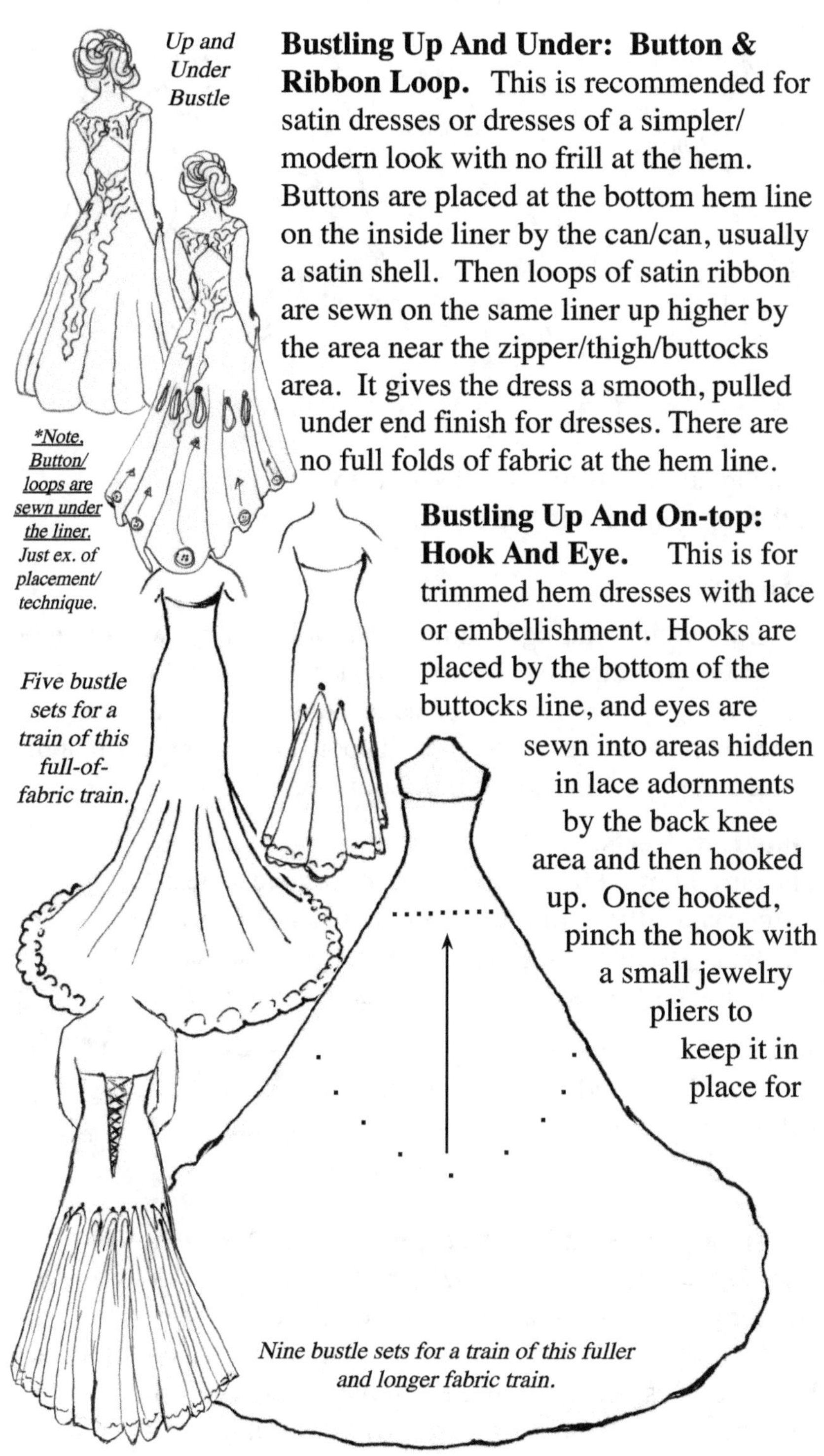

Bustling Up And Under: Button & Ribbon Loop. This is recommended for satin dresses or dresses of a simpler/modern look with no frill at the hem. Buttons are placed at the bottom hem line on the inside liner by the can/can, usually a satin shell. Then loops of satin ribbon are sewn on the same liner up higher by the area near the zipper/thigh/buttocks area. It gives the dress a smooth, pulled under end finish for dresses. There are no full folds of fabric at the hem line.

Bustling Up And On-top: Hook And Eye.   This is for trimmed hem dresses with lace or embellishment. Hooks are placed by the bottom of the buttocks line, and eyes are sewn into areas hidden in lace adornments by the back knee area and then hooked up. Once hooked, pinch the hook with a small jewelry pliers to keep it in place for

dancing later. This gives a nice draped look at the top with lots of full layers at the bottom.

Shoes

Consider your wedding location: Will it be sandy, will there be wet grass, will there be a slippery concrete or wood floor? These things and other surface conditions can have a great effect on how well certain types of footwear will perform and, therefore, what footwear will be suitable.

Flats/Low Heels:
The current trend favors flats or comfortable shoes:
• Moccasins • Running Shoes • Ballet Flats • Canvas
• Cowgirl Boots • Sculpted Flip-Flops *(just add a strap to heel/ankle to stop that 'flip/flop' sound going down the aisle if needed)*, etc.

Heels For Many Reasons:
•If needed to avoid hem alterations.
• If useful to adjust height relative to the groom.
• If you just love those stylish heels!

Changing Shoes At The Reception... And You Want To Avoid Bustling The Front Of The Gown?   Try to find a similar heel height so as not to trip on the dress hem at the dance. Look for a big straight-across platform sandal of same heel height as you wore at the ceremony for comfort. If you go from heeled shoes to flats ... you will be walking and tripping on the front of the dress while the back of the dress is neatly bustled. You can pick up your dress with your hands all night... but it may be inconvenient if you want to drink or just have a free hand as you walk, talk and dance.

Get yourself some washable silicone shoe pad inserts. They are awesome and stick easily into any heeled shoe in your closet for future re-use! Easy to wash and re-use.

Beware of glittered shoes or shoes with 'rough' bling. Try them on with the dress, some shoes 'snag' or 'catch' the hems, which can cause tripping. If you gotta have those shoes, maybe spray paint or do by hand a few thin coats of clear gloss paint to 'smooth out' the texture.

Keeping the shoes on, add some silicone inserts to keep your feet happy for the big long day and night. They are washable and reusable for years.

Reception/dance heel change, go to the platform flip-flop to keep you from stepping on your dress. Lets your feet get comfy.

Jewelry Suggestions

Just some tips to keep things easy. Some dresses need jewelry, while some need very little, if any, to compliment the gown.

Metals. Try to match any metals in the dress. If there are antique metal diamond studs and thread, then go for dark/antique metal jewelry. Bright silver thread on a dress would call for bright silver jewelry. Gold for gold.

Pearls. Try on pearls, many pearl shades are available, find the one that matches your dress best. Are the pearls stark white or cream or antiqued?

Bracelet. Go for a repeated pattern bracelet. It will involve less maintenance for you during photos. The heavy centered embellishment will eventually slide to the inside of your wrist than out to the photographer. Otherwise, remember you are holding a bouquet in most photos, which could hide the bracelet.

Necklace Length. Try them on! Don't let the necklace fall into the chest of the dress. But it should not be so short that it lays on the outline of your collarbone and makes the necklace chain look 'wavy' on you.

Think of this jewelry purchase as an heirloom to add to your collection, not just something for the wedding day. Find unique local pieces that you "love". Heirloom jewelry pieces are an option too. Ask grandma, mom, aunt, etc.

Try on the jewelry with the dress before ceremony.

Tan Lines Are you a lifeguard? Whatever the reason for being outside, you likely have serious tan lines if you spend significant time outside.

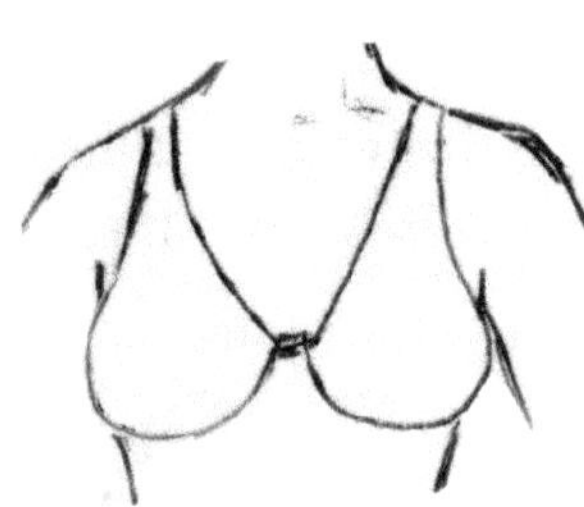

Swimesuit lines lines in this shape?

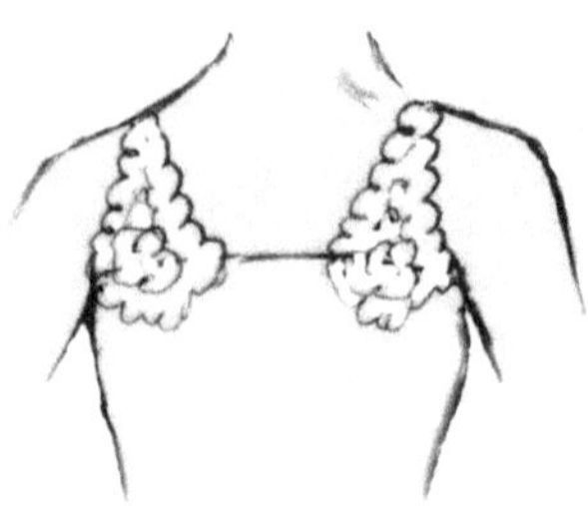

Try covering up the tanlines with lace embellishments.

COVERAGE OPTIONS:
• Try to find a style of dress with straps to cover the lines or make straps in the same positions on the dress as where the lines are so as to cover them. Or cover up the lines with complimentary lace/sheer fabric in the same shape as the lines.
• Bolero, shawl or some cover-up.
• Spray tan - try it first. Buff the skin well, let it dry well. Have a friend help apply to the untanned areas. If the 'off-shelf' tan is not looking right, then go to a professional spray tan booth, but please give it a test run a good month before your ceremony.
DON'T STRESS - There is Photoshop to fix your digital pictures!

Veils And Hair Candy!

Hair Candy!

Flowers • Tiara • Broach Pin • Scarf • Decorated Bobbi Pins • Vintage Hat • Hats Of All Kinds • Ribbons •   Veils!
Styles are: Birdcage, top of dress/shoulder, below zipper, thigh length, floor length or cathedral length. Fabrics include plain tulle, shimmery tulle, swiss dot tulle, sheers and more. Some are trimmed with lace, beads or no trim.

**Save even more money by creating your own veil, try it with a friend or family member who dabbles in quilting/sewing because they will have a rotary cutter and matt board. I believe you can do it. The bottom end of tulle is cut at a curve with a rotary cutter on a matt board. Then the tulle is gathered at the opposite end and attached to a plastic haircomb with thread by hand sewing it through the comb ends. Cover up the gathering by putting some 'bling' on top by sewing or using a hot glue gun. Voila, you are done.*

Showcase your hair your way!

Explore all the fabric options of swiss dot to checked to patterned tulle options, sheers and more.

OH NO.... OH NO....

MY DRESS DOESN'T FIT!

LIFE HAPPENED AND YOU GAINED WEIGHT!

Your dress is too small! Way too small! What Can You Do?

Do A Small Diet Change! Almost No Exercise Needed.

Do These Things And You Can Lose 3 To 5 Inches Around Your Waist In One Month!

Bride's Part:

Eat Breakfast: Have breakfast. Eat a protein (chia seeds, egg, peanut butter) and a healthy carbohydrate (creamy buckwheat cereal) with fruit. Avoid sugary processed cereal. *Buckwheat is not wheat.*

Carbohydrate Shift: Avoid gluten (wheat). N o white pasta; eat gluten free pasta, I like brown rice pasta best. Try quinoa as a substitute. Avoid white rice ; eat brown rice. Try wild rice, it's great with mushrooms and onions. Try gluten free recipes on the internet.

Focus On Veggies & Protein! Pre-cut a lot of veggies. You really will be more likely to eat them if they are on hand for snacks and meal time. Steam, not boil, your veggies if possible to retain all nutrients and fiber. Eat unprocessed meats, eggs, cheese, nuts, peanut butter, beans or quinoa for protein.

Beverage Change: No wine and no sweet beverage of any form *including diet sodas*. Use honey, stevia leaf (1 fresh leaf is great in tea cup) or maple syrup for a sweetener.

**Avoid high-fructose corn syrup in all packaged foods if possible. Corn syrup/sugar calories are a huge culprit for gaining weight and retaining water.*

Exercise & Stretch: Go for a walk every day. If you can't go outside due to allergies or illness, do yoga. Find a great beginners yoga video and do 20 minutes, or two 10 minute sessions a day. Posture will improve. **I am not a nutritionist. I am gluten intolerant with a few other food allergies. "From my own personal diet experience and other bridal dieters and their results I suggest this plan." You c   an find scientific discussions on NPR. You may wish to consult your doctor or other qualified professional (e.g., registered dietician) before making any serious change to your diet.*

Seamstress Part:

Let Out Seams As Much As Possible.   Gowns can typically have 1" to 4" total of extra fabric at the side seams to let out. However, lace embellished dresses typically do not have any extra lace at the hip/thigh/knee side seams.

Add A Corset!   Remove the top portion of the zipper and install the corset loops/boning/satin back panel/ribbon.

**This is the extent of what the seamstress can do about your dress size dilemma.*

Bridesmaid

Special Ordering Of Gowns.   Go by the manufacturer's size chart. Size can vary between different countries and different manufacturers.

**Have your body measurements taken at the bridal shop.... see what the tape measure is saying at your chest, waist & hips and sign off on those*

One-strap - Empowering. This asymetrical look is one of the most universal styles that flatters almost every body type. You still have a somewhat strapless look, but with the confidence of having a strap for support. Plus, the strap helps hold up the dress if the chest fit is slightly loose. That means one less alteration.

One-strap gowns come in a variety of styles. A choice dress for the entire wedding party.

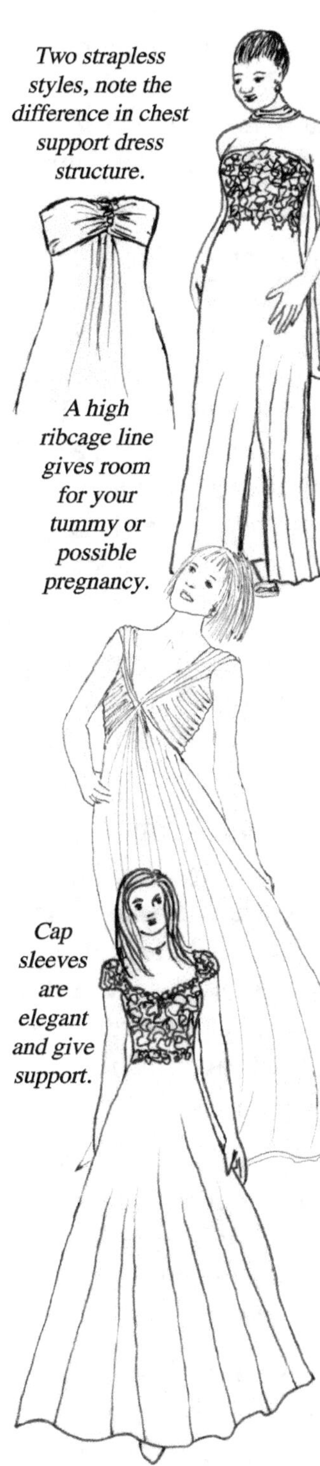

Strapless -   Structured. There are many versions of the strapless dress with varying amounts of structure. In this style it is good to consider your bridesmaid's chest size. Women with ample chests are typically not excited at the prospect of keeping up a strapless dress. Extra boning and stabilizing options are available, but that means extra cost to your bridesmaid and sometimes results in more uncomfortable pressure points in the dress. And for women who are 'flat', the only option for most styles is to fill up the chest with cups. Some women are not comfortable in 'growing' a chest overnight. The chest curves may be sewn back to a better fit if style permits.

Goddess/Empire Waist - Timeless. A good dress option for many reasons: Room to cover any tummy rolls, or if you're pregnant and need the room for growth. However, many goddess gowns are very full at the hem and can have many layers, which is more costly if the gown needs to be hemmed and/or is up to four layers deep! Try on the knee length goddess dress to avoid hem alterations.

Lace Cap Sleeve -   Very elegant. Hides armpit 'pooching' and adds to the shoulder line. Helps to hold up a dress and avoid chest seam alterations if the dress is slightly

loose at the chest. Some alterations, such as darts in the shoulder blade area, are typically needed to keep a 'smooth back' look for petite women.

Ruched - Dimensional. All the ruching folds give dimension to the dress. A good covering dress for hiding rolls. Whether you have rolls or not, all women think they do, and they all see more than what is really there. So this is also a dress to help those who are less confident about their body. It also adds nice visual lines to the gowns for movement in photos.

A-Line Dress - A classic. Great for a windy outdoor wedding. It's the least expensive to alter for hems as it is not as full as many other styles.

Knee Length Gowns - Flirty and fun. Typically less expensive than floor length. Research if the dress is available in petite if anyone in the wedding party is petite. A small extra fee for petite may apply, however, the fee is usually cheaper than hemming charges.

Avoid choosing a very full width, short skirt dress if you're going to be getting married in a windy environment. In that event, go for a tighter styled gown.

Pregnant Bridesmaid - The goddess/empire (high-waist style) dress has room for pregnancy. There

23

is room for the growing baby bump. A short hem dress is also more cool to wear in a hot outdoor wedding. This could be a huge cost savings on alterations for women about to give birth, or who have recently given birth.

Train - Fashionable, but will need a bustle after the ceremony is over. Otherwise, it is a trip hazard when dancing or walking around because guests and children are milling around too.

Sequin - Flashy. The shine is great. Sequins are great for travel because the dress hardly wrinkles! However, under arms may get tender if there are too many sharp edged sequins rubbing. Plus, if the bridesmaid has any bumps or rolls the shine of the sequins on the dress accentuates this greatly.

Alteration charges can vary as some dresses can be sewn by machine, and some only by hand. The sequins can have thick plastic that the sewing machine cannot punch through, so they must be sewn by hand. Work done by hand takes more time and thus increases cost.

Deep belly button? Fill it in with a cotton ball, then a cosmetic pad and seal position with tape or bandaid.

**Hide the 'inny' bellybutton hole by taping in cotton balls into the bellybutton if needed to smooth out the dress.*

**Some of the happiest bridesmaids are those for whom the bride specified color and/or designer, leaving the bridesmaid to chose the style! She picked the gown she would feel most beautiful in, which gives confidence, comfort and results in a great photo!*

Color For The Bridesmaid

My comments about color are just suggestions. I am an artist as well as a seamstress, and I love color. I have never met a color that I could not love in the correct setting. However, please consider that your bridesmaid is probably buying her dress to honor you. Consider skin tones, photography and scenery. If you gotta have bright colors or flourescent, try using them as accents or in the flowers. These are my suggestions.

Jewel Tones Are The Best -   Jewel tones are the best for most people, especially for a very diverse bridesmaid party. Bright colors are most difficult to make flattering for all the bridesmaids. Pastels can be great, but they do wash out some people.

Consider The Photography Scenery - Beige can be great and it can be awful! Beware the beige dress that looks like you're naked! Beware of a beige dress on the beige beach, because too much blending into the scenery will look odd in photos. The background is important. Teal/blue sky on a beach with teal/blue dresses results in the people looking like floating heads, arms and legs on a beach. Green dresses in the green grass with green trees has a similar result. Tan in a desert background or black in a poorly lit venue that does not allow flash photography also result in unsatisfactory photos.

Saving Money For The Bridesmaid Through Less Alterations

Saving On Hem And Bust - Consider a knee length dress with one shoulder strap. Short dresses are usually less expensive at the bridal shop. Short dresses also are less full, so if a hem is still needed, the alteration costs less. The one shoulder strap option is also a universally flattering option if you want the same style of dress for bridesmaids of differing shapes and sizes. The one shoulder strap can also be just enough

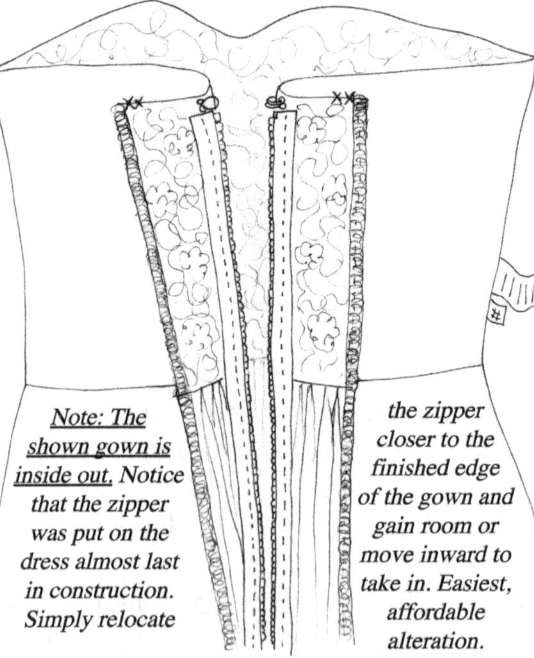

to keep up the dress if it is just slightly loose around the chest to avoid side seams being taken in, as a strapless dress must fit like a glove to keep it up. That results in most bridesmaids needing less alterations!

Save By Letting Out Sides By Back Zipper Relocation Instead Of Side Seams

** Check The Zipper Construction On The Back Along The Spine Of The Dress. Only Available On Some Styles.*

If the gown needs to be let out only 1-4" and the zipper is up the back and sewn on top of a finished dress... you can just move the zipper in to seam edges along the back seams gaining up to 1"-3" in the chest and waist area. This avoids the need to adjust two lined side seams and waist, which makes for a less expensive alteration.

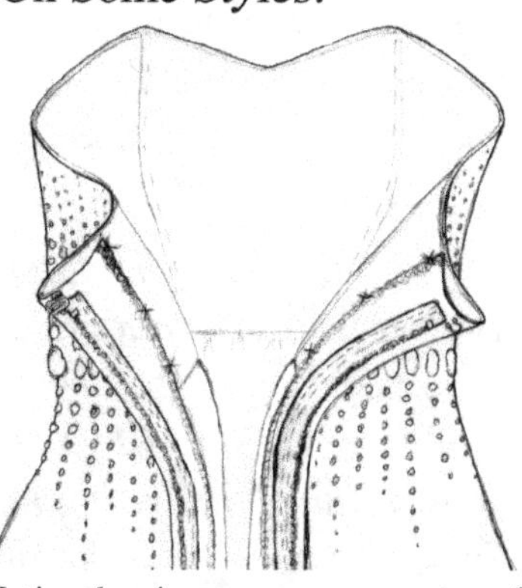

**Notice the zipper was sewn on-top of the gown last in construction order. Relocate the zipper for a better fit. Easiest, affordable alteration.*

Jr. Bridesmaid

Please consider your junior bridesmaid's age, height (any possibility of growth spurt?), body development, and confidence level. Youth dress sizes are limited. Some styles are more for a youth with a mostly grown woman's body.

Strapless -   This is not a dress that she would typically wear. Most young girls do not have the rib cage and hip development to hold up a strapless dress. Many alterations will probably be necessary to keep this kind

Girls develop at all rates. Curvy dresses may need lots of alterations. Also, girls do not always have the hips yet to help keep up a strapless dress.

of dress from falling off. The alterations may even include sewing off the chest curves and hip curves on all layers of the dress, as most dresses are created with the idea that all girls have a chest and hips. However, every girl grows at a different rate. Sewing off the excess chest is possible with some styles, but not all, and then cups may be necessary to stop the dress from caving in to her chest. A quick fix is to consider having straps added to the dress. Use Photoshop to erase out the straps in your wedding photos if you like.

About 80% of girls under age 13 have cried or had an irritated, almost hostile response about a strapless style dress during the fitting. Most mothers were unaware until the fitting about how the girl really felt.   An unhappy or uncomfortable junior bridesmaid makes for a sad photo.

Shoes - Flats or 1/2" heel are advisable. Your junior bridesmaid is already going to be challenged by a long day of walking in a full dress.

Dress Dilema -   If you can't find a junior/girls bridesmaid's dress that fits appropriately, then try looking for a dress of complimentary color in a fine department store. Some dresses can be ordered in colors other than what is on the floor. Holidays, homecoming, winter dances and spring prom are great times to look with a larger selection typically being available.

Girls develop at all rates, physically and mentally.
Consider the girl's physique and personality when selecting the gown.

Mother

Mothers look great in photos when they are comfortable and feel beautiful in their gown. Have fun with her and try on many styles. Find what she likes and then start taking photos. Go to bridal shops, boutiques, department stores, etc. and give it a week at least see what dress is still on your mind.

Color: Consider having the mother not match your wedding party exactly. Guests may get confused . Go for a complimentary color or tone to be flattering to her and your wedding party.

Jacket, Bolero, Shawl can be decorated with a broach....etc. Satin, lace, knits and bias cut linen are some of the many fabrics in which you can find these cover-ups.

Many mothers will want to wear a gown with some sleeve. Explore all the bolero styles if sleeves are not available.

Most mothers do not like the looks of their arms. Find the arm cover-up first, and then find her dress if she is concerned about her arms. Some gowns have a matching bolero/jacket but many do not. *It is easier to find the jacket first and a gown to match later.*

Mom Gone Flashy Wild? - Did a mother go wild with her fashion ideas? Don't stress it. Present her a gift of a bolero or shawl to tone down the flashy gown. Otherwise you can use arrangements, your husband or your bouquet as a "close-up cover-up" photo strategy if that dress is just too loud. You can also use Photoshop on the computer to tone down the color saturation of the dress in a photo if you must. Finally, you are the one who gets to choose which photos are hung in your home and which stay in the photo album.

Flower Girl

Consider her age and if she could have a growth spurt. Get shoes that let her walk, dance and run comfortably because that is what little girls do.   Get a dress that both compliments you and reflects her taste in fashion. She will be more enthusiastic about wearing it and will likely smile even more

Expect a few interesting expressions in your photos if the dress is uncomfortable or itchy. For example: lots of big satin flowers around the neckline may look cute, but she will not like to wear a dress with flowers that come up to her chin. Also, too many beads under the armpit area will rub and hurt. Glitter may come off and onto her hands, creating a need to wash hands a lot.

Ring Bearer

Tux sizes for little boys are limited. If renting is not an option, then purchase a suit, or retro paper boy outfit, or dress shirt and dress pants ensemble.

Shop around Easter or other holidays when the selection will be best in stores.

Vests, hats, ties, bow ties, belts, cowboy boots, etc. are great accessories to jazz up pants and shirt.

Remember that most boys will remove their suit/tux jacket, tie, and/or vest as soon as they can after the ceremony.

Groom

Formal wear of tuxes and suit sizes are determined by both size and style. The Groom needs to look at the various styles and try them on to see what he likes best. Some styles are very fitted. Some are boxy. Some are in between. What style fits the best and has comfort of ease to move in is what he should pick. Very muscular men are not going to be able to move comfortably in very fitted tuxes and there could be last minute size issues.

Once the tux is selected, be sure to order it at least three months in advance. Rented formalwear typically include a jacket, vest, shirt, neckwear, cufflinks, pants and shoes. Your traveling groomsmen should have their measurements taken at their local formalwear store or seamstress and the measurements should be sent to your store.

Anther option is to wear a suit. Have all the men wear their black or gray or navy suit. Make sure the groomsmen try on their suits two months before the wedding. All should wear either black shoes or brown shoes for continuity. A suit is a great investment. Suits range from $100 to $500 on average. A tux is around $120 and up to rent.

Miscellaneous

Website Garment Purchasing — - I highly recommend you purchase from reputable sites. BE ADVISED that many knock-off dresses are not comparable to designer gowns. The quality of fabric, craftsmanship and construction are lacking. Many times I have seen gowns that barely resembled the example, or that were of poor quality, wrong color, wrong size or had some other problem. Return postage is costly, and the item may not be trackable if it is international. There is no guarantee you'll get your money back or a replacement dress in time.

Invitations

E-invites vs. Paper Mail Invites: Do Both!

E-Invites, including social media, have their place for the bachelor/bachelorette parties. Paper invitations are still the recommended way. Not everybody has or checks social media regularly.

Paper invites are still highly recommended for showers and are a must for the actual wedding ceremony. Everyone loves the reminder on the fridge, it is essential to all age levels for different reasons.

Outside Venue? Please indicate so in the invitation. Consider notifying your invitees of the need for sunscreen or jackets and how many layers of clothing your guests might need for absolute comfort.

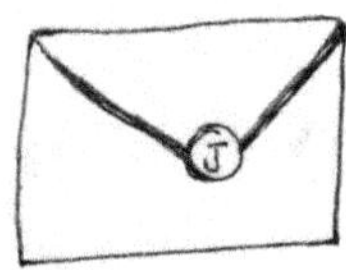

If you think sending just e-invites is fine, think again. I have heard many complaints about that procedure for all sorts of reasons and from people of differing ages.

Church/Venue Considerations

FASHION: Find out ahead of time if the officiant has any dress requirements. This tends to depend on the officiant, so be sure to ask so to avoid the necessity of last minute "additions" to your dress for the ceremony.

Some examples that have arisen include.... the need for cap sleeves, gowns could not expose the shoulders. Another is that the gown could be strapless, but not show flesh 2" below the collar bone.

Wedding Ceremony Program: Can you design and get it printed? Can only the church/venue design and print it? Or can you design it and you then can print them, after the officiant proofreads and approves of it?

Flowers/Cake/Alcohol/Food: Some venues will let outside vendors bring in their creations. Other venues have you sign contracts that you will only buy from them, and might specify a minimum dollar amount too.

ASK QUESTIONS. Keep it simple.
Get your obligations in writing.

Holiday Weddings

Holidays are one of the few guaranteed & possibly paid days off that many family and friends enjoy. Please be sure you are not infringing on their long-planned time off. Also, florists are very busy at holidays, ask about availability.

Destination Weddings

These can be exciting and fun to combine with your honeymoon time. They are also a good way to make your ceremony more intimate with a smaller guest list. Sounds like fun. But please consider that it can be a considerable financial or time burden for invitees. Be sure all the wedding party members are financially able to afford time off from work, the airplane ticket, hotel and food, wedding attire, shoes and accessories and gifts. Also, guests may feel pressure to come and others will be distressed that they cannot afford to come. However, if you want an intimate ceremony then this may be the way to do it without telling your large family/friend network that you just want a few guests and no more.

Having a hot beach wedding? Wear a tea length hem or shorter for air flow. Or wear a gown of cool silk or linen. Polyester is not a breathing fabric like silk or linen.

Measurements

Take your measurements. Know your size and try to keep close to it. Avoid extra desserts, wine or extreme dieting before your wedding or you will have many alterations.

Sizing idea. Not sure about the sizing and there is no sample dress in any size to try on? Try on the same designer's dresses of similar fitted styles. This will give you an idea of cut and size of the dress.

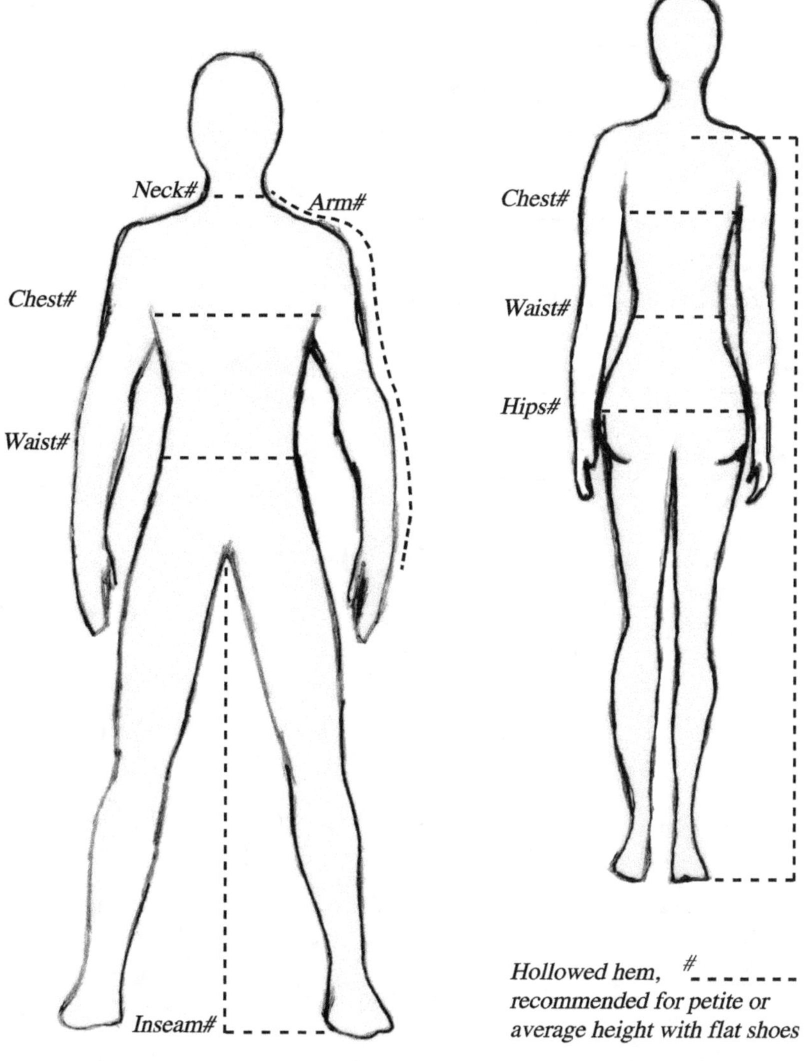

Tux/Suit Notes

Designer Model#/Name   How did it fit/feel? Cost$

____

____

____

____

____

____

____

____

____

____

Put on the garment and take a picture, look at it again later.

Knowing what to be aware of
makes choosing a gown simpler
and less stressful. Because sewing
skills are typically no longer
taught in school or in the home,
I have prepared this guide to help
make your choice in styles easier.
This should save you money.

Kay Brandt

At Your
Bridal Fitting
DON'T FORGET TO BRING
Your Shoes,
the bra you might wear,
and jewelry too.

Can't Decide?

THIS GUIDE WILL HELP!

Tips for the entire wedding party.

Every garment needs some little alteration.

Bustling and enforcing hooks.

www.ingramcontent.com/pod-product-compliance
Lightning Source LLC
Chambersburg PA
CBHW060819260726
48660CB00003B/1005